TAYLOR LAUTNER

OVERNIGHT SIZZLIN' SENSATION

SIMON PULSE
An imprint of Simon & Schuster Children's Publishing Division
1230 Avenue of the Americas, New York, NY 10020
First Simon Pulse paperback edition October 2009

For information about special discounts for bulk purchases, please contact
Simon & Schuster Special Sales at 1-866-506-1949 or business@simonandschuster.com.
Designed by Simon Davis
Manufactured in the United States of America
2 4 6 8 10 9 7 5 3 1
Library of Congress Control Number 2009934855
ISBN 978-1-4424-0368-0

TAYLOR LAUTNER

OVERNIGHT SIZZLIN' SENSATION

AN UNAUTHORIZED BIOGRAPHY BY MEL WILLIAMS

Simon Pulse　New York　London　Toronto　Sydney

INTRODUCTION

He's cuter than Zac, fitter than Corbin, and more talented than the Jonas brothers put together—the hot new star in Hollywood is Taylor Lautner! A martial arts champion since the age of seven, and an in-demand actor since he was eight, Taylor has hit the big-time as gorgeous Jacob Black in the blockbuster saga *Twilight*. Want to find out what's behind the smoldering dark good looks and muscled torso? For instance, is Taylor aloof and big-headed or friendly and down-to-earth? What does he do to stay so fit? What kinds of girls does he like? What hopes does he have for the future? For the answers to these and many other questions, just read on. This book will tell you what Taylor Lautner is really like, inside and out.

QUICK TAYLOR QUIZ

Q) *Twilight* was nominated for twelve awards at the Fox Teen Choice Awards in August 2009. Which award did Taylor win?

A) Fresh Male Face.

Taylor fact file

Full name: Taylor Daniel Lautner

Birthplace: Grand Rapids, Michigan

Date of birth: February 11, 1992

Star sign: Aquarius

Height: 5 feet 10 inches

Eyes: Deep brown—like chocolate!

Hair: Black (and strokeable!)

Ethnic origin: French, Dutch, German, and Native American descent

Parents: Daniel and Deborah Lautner

Siblings: One younger sister, Makena

Pets: A Maltese dog named Roxy

Home: Los Angeles, California

Taylor's early years

Taylor was born on February 11, 1992, to Dan and Deborah Lautner, who lived on Rosewood Avenue in Grand Rapids, Michigan. Both their families lived in Michigan too, so little Taylor was surrounded by loving relatives as he grew up. Taylor's mom had a job at an office furniture design company and Taylor's dad was a commercial airline pilot. Whenever he was at home, father and son loved playing ball games together and watching sports on TV—especially football, basketball, and wrestling. Tiny Taylor was soon completely crazy about all sports and decided at a very early age that he wanted to be a professional athlete when he grew up.

One night when Taylor was four, the family's home caught fire and burned down—very fortunately, none of them were in it, as Taylor's dad was away on a flight and Taylor and his mom had gone to stay with an aunt. The Lautners lost most of their possessions and had to start all over again.

They went to live in Hudsonville, Michigan. The new house was bigger than their old one, which was lucky because, when Taylor was six, his sister Makena came along.

Fast fact

Taylor has always had a big imagination. As soon as his sister, Makena, was old enough to play with him, he liked creating games of "pretend"— especially acting out being spies and secret agents.

The karate kid

Taylor's mom had a work friend who took his sons to karate lessons, and she wondered if Taylor might like to try it too. Of course, her sports-mad son was in his element and loved it right away. In an interview with karateangels.com, Taylor later said, "I really liked class because of all the games we got to play like Swords and Spears, Sensei Says, etc." However, his instructor, Tom Fabiano, remembers the classes differently—he saw that Taylor was dedicated and pushed himself, and he realized right away that the six-year-old was something special. "A lot of boys that age are bouncing off the walls, but Taylor was always deliberate, focused," he said. "He wasn't a typical kid. He always worked extra hard." Taylor took to karate so fast that, after just one year, Fabiano thought he should enter a national competition. Taylor won three first-place trophies, at only seven years old!

Taylor says . . .
"From karate, I've [always] had the drive and confidence to push myself. . . ."

An extreme experience

Present at the national karate competition was top martial artist and actor Mike Chat—also known as the Blue Power Ranger on the kids' TV show *Power Rangers Lightspeed Rescue*. World karate champion Mike couldn't help but notice little Taylor's outstanding performance. He was so impressed that he invited Taylor to attend a summer training camp in Los Angeles for an amazing sport he had created called XMA, which stands for "extreme martial arts." This is a blend of kickboxing, tae kwon do, yoga, ballet, and acrobatics, which features

Taylor's favorite party trick!

breathtaking stunts, leaps, kicks, and flips. Taylor later told the *Grand Rapids Press*, "I fell in love! By the end of the camp I was doing aerial cartwheels with no hands!" Mike was delighted and offered to continue to train Taylor. From then on, the Lautners found themselves regularly flying off to LA so that Taylor could attend specially arranged training sessions with Mike. Mike was a hard taskmaster: He also gave Taylor XMA homework to do back in Michigan. Taylor didn't mind the tough schedule—in fact, he loved it!

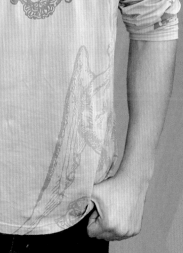

Taylor's smile is just as cute now!

QUICK TAYLOR QUIZ

Q) At which venue was the XMA summer camp attended by Taylor held?

A) The University of California in Los Angeles (known as UCLA).

Following in a star's footsteps

By the time Taylor was eight, he had gained his karate black belt, won three gold medals at the World Karate Association Championships in the twelve-and-under division (becoming Junior World Forms and Weapons Champion), and joined Mike Chat's elite XMA performance and competition squad, Team Chat International. He was also training for other sports he enjoyed, keeping up with his friends, and gaining top grades at school—Taylor told karateangels.com, "I get mostly As with an occasional A- here and there." Phew!

As if all that wasn't enough, screen star Mike Chat suggested that Taylor try acting, too. Taylor later told an interviewer with the *Grand Rapids Press*, "He saw that I wasn't shy, that I was confident, that I talked a lot." And of course, because of his XMA one-on-one training sessions with Mike, Taylor was regularly flying to Los Angeles, the home of Hollywood. Mike helped Taylor get a showbiz agent, who set up auditions for him whenever he was in LA. The first audition Taylor went to was for a Burger King commercial—despite his incredible cuteness he didn't get the part, as they were looking for someone older. But Taylor wasn't put off—in fact, he was bitten by the showbiz bug.

QUICK TAYLOR QUIZ

Q) What's the name of the school Taylor attended till he was eleven?

A) Jamestown Elementary School in Hudsonville, Michigan.

INTO THE SPOTLIGHT

In 2001, nine-year-old Taylor won his first acting role—and in something much more exciting than a Burger King commercial: a part in a martial-arts action movie for TV called *Shadow Fury*. Set in the future, when cloning has become a routine procedure, *Shadow Fury* tells the story of the struggle against mad scientist Dr. Oh, who learns how to control clones' minds and also creates a ninja clone called Takeru who is the ultimate human killing machine. Taylor played a "good" clone character called Kismet, and although he was only in the movie for a short time—he played Kismet as a child—he got to show off his dazzling martial arts skills in a dramatic fight scene where he kills one of the bad guys. Playing a hero ninja must have been a dream come true for little Taylor.

Fast fact

When Taylor was nine, he competed in the seventeen-and-under age group in the World Karate Association Tournament in Chicago and won the Warrior Trophy Cup. He then took a year off from martial arts competitions and enjoyed spending more time playing football, basketball, and baseball, and going horseback riding.

Taylor hits HOLLYWOOD

With his incredible cuteness, dazzling martial arts skills, and natural acting ability, Taylor's appearance in *Shadow Fury* brought him to the attention of many Hollywood movie-makers. He was soon in such demand for auditions that he was flying to LA a couple of times a month. "They'd call at nine or ten at night, which was six or seven their time and say, 'We've got an audition tomorrow, can you be here?'" Taylor once said. "We'd leave really early in the morning and get there about noon. I'd go to the audition in the afternoon, take the red-eye back to Grand Rapids, then go to school."

Taylor ended up doing so much traveling that, when he was ten, the family thought they'd try living in LA for a month. Taylor went for lots of auditions, but didn't land any parts. On the Lautners' very last day, Taylor got a callback. "That gave me the drive to keep going," he said. The family extended their stay to six months and Taylor continued to audition. Finally, he heard he was going to voice a character in a *Rugrats Movie* commercial. Spurred on, Taylor told his parents he didn't want to move back to Michigan, he wanted to stay and give acting his best shot. The Lautners made the difficult decision to leave behind all their relatives and friends and move to LA for good.

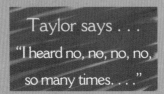

Taylor says . . .
"I heard no, no, no, no, so many times. . . ."

16

Born to perform

Taylor soon realized that he didn't just love performing on-screen as an actor, he enjoyed any sort of activity where he was in the limelight! During 2003, while throwing himself into audition after audition, he also stayed a member of the XMA Performance Team, putting on supercool displays at martial arts competitions, sportswear shops, and professional basketball games. Taylor took dance lessons too—and was soon so good that he joined two performance groups: LA Hip Kids (a hip-hop dance crew) and Hot Shots (a jazz dance group). He even took voice lessons and had great fun recording a few songs with his friends. Taylor was a natural, all-around performer.

By the time Taylor was eleven, he had done countless acting auditions—and was finally starting to have great success. In 2003 he guest-starred on a well-known comedy TV program, *The Bernie Mac Show*. Taylor played a bully called Aaron—a part nothing like himself in real life—but was thrilled by the whole TV experience and soon got to do more. The following year Taylor acted in an episode of the hit teen TV drama *Summerland*, an episode of a comedy series called *My Wife and Kids*, then a role with pop stars Nick Lachey and Jessica Simpson on their program *The Nick and Jessica Variety Hour*. Taylor was fast becoming a seasoned TV actor!

Fast fact

Taylor still loves to use his martial arts and stunt experience. On the set of *New Moon*, he was doing every stunt he could possibly get his hands on!

Among the many auditions Taylor landed were voiceover jobs for commercials and radio jingles. When he was thirteen, this voice work really took off. First Taylor voiced a cartoon character on a Nickelodeon animated series called *Danny Phantom*, which was about a boy who turns into a ghost whenever he wants. Taylor was a pirate ghost called Youngblood.

"He's a lot of fun," he told the *Oregon Herald*. Taylor then did voice work on a Cartoon Network show he was actually a fan of—*Duck Dodgers*, in which Daffy Duck is a futuristic superhero traveling through space. Next, Taylor voiced a character in an episode of the classic cartoon series *What's New, Scooby Doo?* and two episodes of the famous animated series *Peanuts*: "Kick the Football, Charlie Brown" and "He's a Bully, Charlie Brown." Taylor went on to voice leading characters on a Disney dog and cat animated series called *Silas and Brittany* and on the pilot of a cartoon show called *Which Way Is Up?* Work on commercials also continued to roll in—millions of Americans heard Taylor on commercials for products such as Kellogg's Frosted Flakes, Sunkist, Superfresh, Petsmart, and Legoland.

Taylor says . . .

"I love voiceover because you're not on camera and usually you're playing a person totally opposite of yourself and you just get to change your voice and be a weird character—and that's an awful lot of fun."

21

A role WITH BITE

In the midst of all this voiceover work, thirteen-year-old Taylor jumped at the chance to audition for a part in a movie for the big screen. The film was a superhero action flick called *The Adventures of Sharkboy and Lavagirl*, directed by Robert Rodriguez—the famously creative filmmaker behind the Spy Kids movies. Taylor was hugely excited—he thought he could show off his martial arts skills as part of Sharkboy's superpowers. He had to go through three nail-biting auditions and a final test where all the auditioning kids were asked to strike a superhero pose. Taylor balanced upside down on one hand with his legs in a split position. Rodriguez asked his seven-year-old son, Racer, who had come up with the initial idea for the movie, who they should choose. Taylor was pointed to and the role was his!

Taylor says . . .
"We freaked out [when I got the role]—my whole family couldn't sleep for a week!"

AN EXCITING EXPERIENCE

Thirteen-year-old Taylor took the challenges of being a Hollywood film star in stride, from spending forty-five minutes in the hair and makeup trailer and then another half an hour getting into his costume each morning, to doing most of his filming in front of a giant blue screen. This type of acting is very demanding because you have to just imagine all the scenery and props, which are put in later by computer. Director Robert Rodriguez also allowed Taylor a lot of creativity with his character—Taylor even choreographed his own fight scene and did his own stunts. On top of all this, he had to do at least three hours of schoolwork every day!

Luckily, Taylor got along brilliantly with his two costars, Cayden Boyd (who played Max) and Taylor Dooley (Lavagirl). They had a riot playing practical jokes on set, and they hung out a lot after filming and on the weekends. Taylor had made some great new friends.

QUICK TAYLOR QUIZ

Q) What was Taylor's favorite scene in the movie?

A) One of them was when he is on a giant cookie, steps in a puddle of chocolate, and then eats it!

Taylor's first big premiere

Taylor was both anxious and excited to see what fans thought of his first performance as a leading man, so attending the LA premiere of *Sharkboy and Lavagirl* in June 2005 was nerve-racking but also thrilling. "Walking the red carpet, you wouldn't believe how many photographers are there," Taylor later told a reporter. "'Taylor, turn over here. Turn to the right. Hold it here. To the

left. Now over here!' It's really crazy on the red carpet, but knowing that it was *your* premiere made it even more fun."

The movie provided Taylor with his first taste of real fame; he soon found that he was being recognized by young fans wherever he went—usually boys. "I just thought it was so cool," said Taylor. "I couldn't believe that people wanted my picture!"

Taylor says . . .
"I'm very sarcastic like Sharkboy!"

Fast fact

Sharkboy director Robert Rodriguez was certain that Taylor was destined for stardom. "It's no surprise to me that he was going to go on to great things," he later commented to MTV News. "We knew it immediately when we saw him."

Taylor arrives at the 2009 MTV Movie Awards

WORKING with the stars

By the time Taylor attended the *Sharkboy and Lavagirl* premiere, he was already shooting his next film—*Cheaper by the Dozen 2*. Taylor was playing alongside several big Hollywood names, including Steve Martin (*Parenthood*, *Father of the Bride*, *The Pink Panther*), Hilary Duff (*Agent Cody Banks*, *The Lizzie McGuire Movie*, *A Cinderella Story*), Carmen Electra (*Baywatch*, *Scary Movie*), and Bonnie Hunt (*Beethoven*, *Jumanji*, *Cars*). Taylor later told the *Grand Rapids Press*, "That's when I stopped looking at movie stars as movie stars, and just looked at them as people."

QUICK TAYLOR QUIZ

Q) In 2006 Taylor also appeared as a character in a TV program—what was

A) Love, Inc., a show about a group of friends running a dating service.

28

Maybe this was because Taylor had become a big-league movie star himself. After *Cheaper by the Dozen 2* had been on release for a while, the number of fans approaching him tripled—and now they were girls!

Taylor Lautner and Taylor Dooley

Fast fact

Cheaper by the Dozen is a comedy movie starring Steve Martin that follows the exploits of the Baker family, which has twelve kids! In the sequel, they meet the Murtaughs, a similarly wacky family with eight kids, one of whom is Taylor!

TAYLOR'S *big break*

Taylor's acting career seemed to be soaring—until his rising star suddenly came down to earth with a bump. He next won a part in what should have been a major show on TV, *My Own Worst Enemy*, acting the soccer-star son of a character played by movie star Christian Slater (*Young Guns II*, *Robin Hood: Prince of Thieves*, *Interview with the Vampire*). Unfortunately, although there was a lot of buzz about the show, it got poor ratings and was canceled after nine episodes.

However, Taylor wasn't too upset because he was already working on a project predicted to be much, much bigger. He had won the part of Jacob Black in the movie *Twilight*.

Fast fact

Twilight focuses on the love triangle of human Bella Swan, vampire Edward Cullen, and werewolf Jacob Black. Kristen Stewart and Robert Pattinson had already been cast as Bella and Edward by the time Taylor auditioned for Jacob. Taylor had to read scenes with Kristen to see if they had chemistry and to prove he had the looks and acting ability to rival Robert's irresistible vampire!

QUICK TAYLOR QUIZ

Q) How many of the *Twilight* books had Taylor read before getting involved with the movie?

A) None! He hadn't heard of *Twilight* until he auditioned.

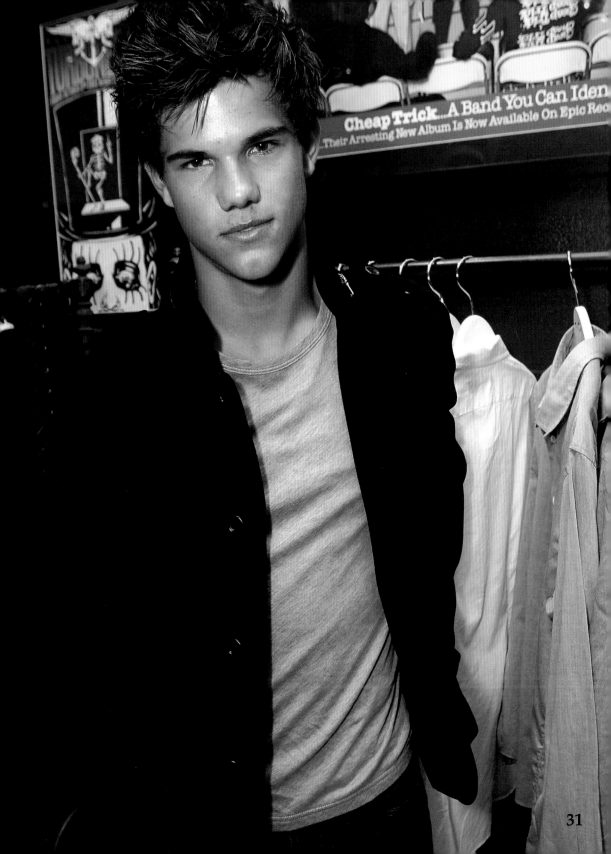

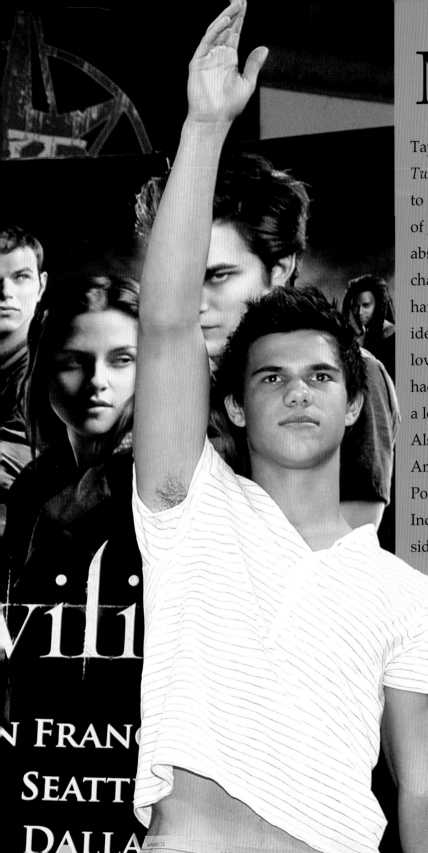

Meet

Taylor pored over the four *Twilight* novels to come to grips with the part of Jacob. He felt he was absolutely cut out for the character. Not only did he have the dark good looks ideal for acting a brooding, lovesick young man, he had the athleticism to play a lean, mean werewolf. Also, Jacob is Native American—Taylor is part Potawatomi and Ottawa Indian on his mother's side. Taylor did research into Jacob's tribe, the Quileute, reading up on their culture and legends, and meeting some tribe members to talk about life on their reservation near Portland.

Jacob Black

The role of Jacob is really very small in the first *Twilight* movie—Taylor was going to be in only three scenes—but he wanted to set up the character exactly right for the following movies, in which Jacob plays a major role.

QUICK TAYLOR QUIZ

Q) Did Taylor grow his hair long for *Twilight?*

A) No. He hated the wig, though—it was itchy and got in the way when he was trying to eat or say his lines!

Taylor says . . .

"I love the character. He has two sides. The first movie shows you his regular boyish side. That side is just like me. He's talkative and fun. In the second book, he transforms into a werewolf. He's grumpy and fierce. He's totally opposite. That challenges me as an actor."

33

A movie phenomenon

Before *Twilight* was released, Taylor told a reporter for movies.about.com, "It's hard not to be nervous when you know there's a few million [*Twilight*] fans out there who are just dying for this movie to come out. . . ." Taylor couldn't believe how *Twilight* fans mobbed him wherever he went. "It's the closest I'll feel to being a rock star," he told one reporter, laughing. Taylor and the cast embarked on a grueling promotions schedule from LA to London to Tokyo to Sydney—personal appearances before hordes of screaming fans, book signings that lasted hours, and endless media interviews. At the July 2008 Comic-Con event in San Diego, eleven thousand fans lined up for autographs! "I don't have time to breathe," Taylor told the *Grand Rapids Press*. "But it's a lot of fun."

Twilight was actually an even more massive success than anticipated. In its first weekend in theaters, it grossed $35.7 million on its opening day and outsold the new James Bond film, *Quantum of Solace*, and *High School Musical 3*. It even set a new record for the biggest opening weekend for a female-directed film. It rocketed to the top of the box offices all around the world.

Fast fact

Taylor was still only sixteen while making *Twilight*. He took his high school tests early, on set, and began to study for college while filming.

THE SAGA CONTINUES

After the success of *Twilight*, all eyes turned to the next film in the saga: *New Moon*. In the book, vampire Edward leaves town and Bella is heartbroken—but her friend, Jacob Black, is there for her . . . harboring desperate unrequited love for Bella, and a hatred for all vampires. Fan opinion was split as to whether Taylor could succeed in bringing Jacob to life in the movie, though. In *New Moon*, Jacob's character develops a darker side, and grows from a baby-faced teenager into a hulking six-foot-seven hunk. Could down-to-earth, naturally lithe Taylor really be convincing?

the twilight saga
new moon

11.20.09

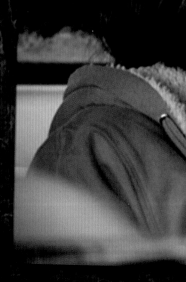

They should have known that Taylor loves a challenge. . . . In the midst of the whirlwind of publicity surrounding *Twilight*, he embarked on a grueling schedule with a personal trainer. He had to build up an incredible thirty pounds of pure muscle. "The hardest thing for me was the eating," Taylor told *Interview*. "I had to shove as much food in my body as possible to pack on calories. My trainer wanted me to do six meals a day and not go two hours without eating. If I would cheat on eating one day, I could tell—I'd drop a few pounds."

TEAM JACOB

Taylor managed an amazing physical transformation.

Many *Twilight* fans are passionately split into two groups according where their loyalties lie: Team Edward (fans who adore the Cullens, a Edward in particular) and Team Jacob (people who think Bella would have been better off with Jacob).

Anticipation was high for Team Jacob as thousands tuned in for the MTV Movie Awards in May 2009 to see a trailer for *New Moon*, and to find out how Taylor would look. Fans were blown away. The clips featured a tantalizing glimpse of the "new" Jacob, naked from the wa up with a six-pack to die for. Another clip featuring those washboar abs teased fans at the 2009 San Diego Comic-Con. Afterward, Taylor told fans that he had worked really hard to portray Jacob well for the The response of six thousand screaming fans proved that Team Jacot had a lot of new support. Not surprisingly, Team Taylor has also nov sprung up!

Taylor says . . .
"It's extremely cool to be part of the *Twilight* project."

Taylor at work

Taylor has always given his all to everything he does—whether it's schoolwork, martial arts, or acting. He knows he is lucky to have landed his dream job and he doesn't take any aspect of it for granted. Taylor never moans about 4:30 a.m. wake-up calls for filming, or grueling publicity schedules. In fact, he chooses to work even harder—he carries a laptop with him because he is taking an online college psychology course. "It's hard . . . but I think it's important, so I try my best to keep up with it," he has said. Taylor knows that the world of showbiz is fickle, and he wants to enjoy every minute of it, do his absolute best, and enjoy developing other aspects of his life too.

Taylor says . . .

"My advice for people that want to act would definitely be, 'You can't get down.' The average booking rate when you're starting is one out of seventy-five auditions—and that's crazy! . . . Once you break into the business more, it will get better. You just can't get down and quit, because it's very, very difficult."

The private Taylor

Despite the immense fame Taylor has found through *Twilight*, he hasn't become stuck-up and big-headed, like many other film stars. "My parents wouldn't allow it," he told one reporter, laughing. "That's not the way they brought me up." Taylor's parents told him he had to stay at school as long as possible so he could be around non-showbiz kids, they give him chores at home, and they only allow him part of his earnings so he learns to live on a budget.

Taylor has loads of showbiz friends, like Taylor Dooley from *Sharkboy and Lavagirl*, Alyson Stoner from *Cheaper by the Dozen 2*, and of course the cast of *Twilight*—who get along really well and enjoy hanging out after filming. But Taylor has also said, "You gotta remember who your friends were before you got famous." In rare time off, he likes nothing better than to get together with either his old school friends or his new showbiz pals to play baseball, basketball, football, or soccer; to go swimming or horseback riding; or just to chill out watching sports on TV.

Taylor's faves

Favorite color	Blue
Favorite food	Steak with A1 sauce
Favorite ice cream flavor	Cake batter
Favorite school subject	PE
Favorite superhero	Spider-Man
Favorite superpower	X-ray vision like Superman
Favorite movie	*The Last Samurai* (starring Tom Cruise)
Favorite actors	Denzel Washington, Brad Pitt, Matt Damon
Favorite TV shows	*American Idol, The Apprentice*
Favorite music artists	OutKast, Black Eyed Peas
Favorite types of food	Mexican and Chinese

Taylor *in Love* 💜

Despite being adored by millions of girls all over the world, Taylor is incredibly modest about his devastating good looks. He once said that the *Twilight* fans are "just passionate for the series and for the characters. . . . I don't think it has much to do with me personally; it's more because I'm playing the beloved Jacob Black." Like any seventeen-year-old boy, Taylor enjoys dating—but he's extremely shy and private when it comes to his love life. When a reporter at the 2009 MTV Music Awards asked if the rumors were true about him dating Disney star Selena Gomez, Taylor actually blushed—all he would say is, "She's a great girl, a great friend." Down-to-earth Taylor has not only been linked to singer Taylor Swift but also Sara Hicks, one of his classmates at Valencia High School—so you don't have to be famous to be his girlfriend! He has said: "The most important quality for me in a girl would probably just be being able to let loose, let go, be a dork and have fun—not to be uptight . . . ."

If you like your chances as the future Mrs. Lautner, here's what else you need to know:

• Do you look like Jessica Alba or Megan Fox? They're Taylor's celebrity crushes.

• Is your zodiac sign Libra, Sagittarius, or Aquarius? They're the signs that Aquarian Taylor is most compatible with.

• Could you put up with Taylor jiggling his knee all the time when he's sitting down? It's his worst habit.

Taylor with Taylor Swift (left) and Kristen Stewart (right)

ONWARD
AND UPWARD

Filming another two movies in the *Twilight* saga will keep Taylor busy for a while, but as one of the rising stars in Hollywood, he's already being lined up for future projects. Taylor wants to branch out into various film genres, to avoid being typecast in the future—so be prepared to see him in some very different movies. One of the first is a romantic comedy called *Valentine's Day*. Taylor's been spotted on set with Taylor Swift, and other stars like Julia Roberts, Ashton Kutcher, and Jessica Alba are all slated to appear in it too.

One day Taylor would love to star in an action-drama like the Bourne movies, which star Matt Damon. And in the future, he also has his eye on writing and even directing.

Outside of acting, he wants to finish studying for his bachelor's degree (and maybe go on to do a master's degree), and keep up with training for his beloved XMA and other sports in his rare time off.

One thing's for certain, though—Taylor's got the looks, the talent, and the drive to be a success at whatever he does. Watch out world, this is only the beginning for superstar Taylor Lautner!